Meant to be Modest

A Call for Women to Return to

Modesty

NICOLE CRONE

Meant to be Modest

Copyright 2016 Nicole Crone

Subject: Christian Living

All Scripture quotations are noted within the text.

Introduction

Hello, friend. Thank you so much for picking up this short book.

I'm a wife and homeschool mama to a bunch of kiddos, who is now in her mid-forties. Walking with God has been the most important thing I have done in my life. Cultivating a close relationship with God has carried me through so much, and I wouldn't change my decision to focus so much of my attention on this very important thing for anything.

Walking with God is one of the best decisions we can make. Truly.

Through the years, this walk has grown deeper as I have grown as a person.

I first wrote this book almost one decade ago, and I'm definitely not quite the same person I was at that time. But I think that is a good thing, and I'm very pleased with my growth…especially my spiritual growth. While writing this edition, a few small things have changed, but at the same time, the heart of the material has stayed the same.

This book is written from a Christian perspective, but I hope it might be helpful to anyone who decides to pick it up. As women, I know we are all trying our best (with God's help, of course) to grow into the best versions of ourselves as possible.

I hope you don't read legalism into the following pages, since this is definitely my intent at all. When I first wrote this book, I was a "skirts only" dresser. While I'm not any longer, I still believe, in general, the best way to present my outward appearance is modestly. There are so many ways to do this, and the good works of God shine forth from me without distraction much easier this way, I think.

At the same time, I realize there are religious male monks who wear very little clothing on purpose, to show solidarity with the poor. In this big wide world, there are many ways to serve God.

In this short book, I've included information about wearing skirts, and even head covering that was in the first edition. I know this was helpful to some of my previous readers, and I'm happy to share my decades-old research with you, even though I look at some things differently nowadays.

I hope you read only love, hope, and encouragement here. Skip chapters that don't apply for you, and please, just look for nuggets of encouragement when something resonates with you.

Modesty is something I wholeheartedly believe that both young and old women should consider as they walk with God. In my experience, when we dress modestly, it is much easier to focus our concentration on our relationship with Him.

But no matter what you decide regarding modesty, you are God's daughter and He will always love you deeply.

In the following pages, you'll find material that I've written on my old blog, along with new information. I plan on touching on the *whys* of modesty, and on topics such as discretion, swimwear, head covering, and more. Near the end of this short book I share my own story. As you read this section, please remember that modesty will look quite different in each family, depending on many individual factors. My hope is that you will walk away with a good understanding as to *why* modesty is important, regardless of how it plays out in your own life. God will give us the grace to make any changes which will ultimately bring us closer to Him.

Blessings,

Nicole

Chapter 1

Modesty isn't Just About What We Wear

I want you to think of a scenario with me.

Imagine that when we wake up, we put on a beautiful, modest outfit. But as soon as we open the bedroom door, we start yelling at our children. Our husband calls us, and we are rude to him since he forgot to take out the trash before leaving for work. We then head to the grocery store, and are really obnoxious to the cashier. If you are a teenager, imagine this same situation but change the characters to include your parents and friends.

Do you think we would be representing God well? Better yet, do you think our relationship with God would be at its best if we did these things?

No.

Despite our modest apparel, our actions would overshadow our attempt to dress modestly.

The definition of modesty is, *"behavior, manner, or appearance intended to avoid impropriety or indecency."* The Bible usually talks about physical clothing when discussing modesty, but it encompasses our behavior and manners also. If our behavior is indecent, our attempts to wear decent clothing will mean nothing to the people we encounter.

As we consider the reasons why we should dress modestly, we must remember that a gentle and quiet spirit is precious to God too! (1 Peter 3:3-4) We cannot forget about this while seeking to please God with our dress.

Modesty is a Form of Holiness

Dressing modesty is a form of holiness. It is a way for us to show our dedication to God tangibly. I will delve into this deeper in just a little bit, but I would love for us to keep the following verse in the front of our minds as we go forward.

"Likewise, I want women to adorn themselves with proper clothing, modestly and discreetly."

1 Timothy 2:9 (NASB)

I believe Paul had good intentions while giving this instruction. (And yes, modesty applies to guys, too.) As I've studied this topic in detail, I've learned we are all meant to be modest. Dressing modestly can be done with a joyful heart, while pointing others to God.

I would like to share an excerpt from a book I read awhile ago. It is called, Dressed to Kill; Thinking Biblically About Modest &

Immodest Clothing by Robert G. Spinney. This is a small excerpt:

*"To be sure, Christians can handle the subject of immodest clothing in a clumsy, unbiblical, and grace-denying fashion. That's a problem. But surely ignoring the subject is not the solution: by doing this, we imply there is no such thing as inappropriate clothing. God's people cannot afford to ignore this issue. Why not? Because Christians who think unbiblically about this issue don't naturally gravitate toward more modest clothing. As is true with other aspects of living the Christian life, we never "drift forward." Holiness and spiritual maturity must be **pursued** (Hebrews 12:14). That pursuit of godliness should be marked by **diligence** (2 Peter 1:10, 3:14). Our mind's default settings are not godly: it is the **renewing** of our minds that produces spiritual transformation. (Romans 12:2).*

Sometimes Christians dismiss the issue of modest clothing as trivial. It's not. After all, it was God who noticed the first clothing ever invented, judged it inadequate, and intervened to replace it with apparel of His own making (Genesis 3:7, 21)."

Pursuing holiness in our dress involves effort, but I've found if we are already pursuing God, it kind of happens naturally. This is great news! We must diligently love God, and try to keep our focus on Him throughout the day. This will keep us on the right path in everything we do, including how we dress.

Our bodies are the temple of the Holy Spirit (1 Corinthians 6:19-20) and we must treat it as such. Think of it this way. We are not only clothing ourselves, but also the Holy Spirit's "home" as well. Our body is a holy dwelling place, and we should dress it accordingly.

Also, women's bodies are in a way inherently holy. Some may say that women contain more of God's essence than men since a

12

new life can form inside of a woman's womb. This "something from nothing" parallels God's ability to create something from nothing in the creation story, and is a very sacred place, whether the woman becomes a mother or not. It is probably good for this holy ground to be kept private and reserved.

As you can tell, I love to talk about this topic. The journey towards holiness is not always easy, but with the Lord's guidance, we can do it, together. In the next few short chapters, I would love to share more about why I believe writing about modesty is so important.

Thoughts to Ponder

- **Are our actions and words good and decent?**
- **If not, what are a few concrete ways we can change our behavior?**

- What are a few ways modest dress can set us apart as daughters of God?
- What are some ways we can keep a quiet and gentle spirit?
- What are a few ways we can pursue holiness?

Chapter 2

Modesty Matters

Once we begin to put God first in our lives, our outward appearance should mirror our inward change. Now, in no way do works produce salvation. I am not suggesting this in the least, and I believe that we are all God's daughters…no matter what. However, once God captures our heart, our desire to please Him and to follow His ways should intensify. Dressing modestly is a biblical way to take attention off of ourselves and point to God instead. If our clothing covers our bodies properly, then the full attention of others will be solely focused on our good works which are bringing glory to God. And isn't giving God glory what life is all about? Modesty will look a bit different to separate individuals, so we need to keep this in mind as we show grace to others.

When we connect with God, the old passes away and we become new. Our worth is now in Christ, and our clothing should reflect that. Our beauty comes from within, and the beautiful light of Jesus should shine through in everything we do. We are daughters of the King, after all!

"The King's daughter is all glorious within."

Psalm 45:13 (KJV)

This is where our focus should be, isn't it? When we take our eyes off of the world's standard of clothing and instead look to God, what's *within* us will shine. Skimpy clothing so easily can detract from this light, and we should really try our best to avoid them.

Why I Write About Modesty

Every once and awhile, someone asks me why I write about modesty, and I'd like to share a few reasons with you right off the bat. They might say, "Isn't there something else you can write about that would better further the kingdom of God?" While there are *many* topics that would take precedence over modesty in order of importance, I believe that God has called *me* to write about *this specifically.* Here are some reasons why I share about modesty:

1. *At one time, I was quite the immodest dresser.* God showed me my error through the Bible and the lives of others. I honestly didn't know that immodesty was a problem that I needed to deal with until I had daughters of my own. The fact that the Lord loves us deeply as daughters, and

that He wants us to dress modestly as a form of protection, has encouraged me to share with those who are on the same path that I used to be on. I'll be sharing my story later!

2. *Modesty is encouraged in God's Word.* 1 Timothy 2:9 says, "Likewise also that women should adorn themselves in respectable apparel, with modesty and self-control..." Instead of just thinking about this verse, it probably would be best to apply it to our lives, too.

3. *Modesty is a form of worship.* It truly is. In 1 Timothy, women are commanded to "likewise" adorn themselves with modesty, as men are to "lift up holy hands." The lifting up of hands is a form of worship, and modesty is too. A bit later, I will devote more time to this topic. Really developing an understanding for this verse helped me to view modesty in a completely different light than I had before.

4. *Our culture is actively immodest as far as clothing is concerned.* If we lived a few hundred years ago, all women generally dressed modestly, since the church's teachings were tied to the government…women had no choice. Now, it is in style to dress immodestly. Oh, how I wish it were not so. Nonetheless, it is so very important to embody God's truth with this current culture.

5. *Since our culture as a whole is immodest, there are not many role models that exhibit modesty.* While I certainly do not consider myself to be a role model, I hope that if I share about modesty, other ladies might not feel alone in this matter.

While modesty is a teaching that we should take very seriously, women most likely *will* apply this to their lives differently. While studying my Bible recently, I came across Romans 14. While Paul is speaking about liberties that we have as Christians, he says that, "The kingdom of God is not eating and drinking, but righteousness and peace and joy in the Holy Spirit...Let us pursue the things which make for peace and the things by which one may edify another. (Romans 14:17, 19 NKJV) We can take the words, "eating and drinking," and replace them with "skirts and pants," or "make up and jewelry." Let's be sure that we do not allow disagreements about such things take our eyes off of what the kingdom of God truly is...love, peace, and joy in God's presence. Thankfully, we can trust God to be our guide as we make clothing choices.

Thoughts to Ponder

- **Does our clothing point others to God, or to ourselves?**
- **What are a few concrete ways we can change our clothing choices to better point to Christ if this is an issue?**

- Do our lives reflect the life we have in God?
- Have we ever used our clothing choices to try and attract attention from men?
- If so, what are a few ways we can return our attention to God?

Chapter 3

Another Reason to Consider Modesty

I desire therefore that the men pray everywhere, lifting up holy hands, without wrath and doubting; in like manner also, that the women adorn themselves in modest apparel, with propriety and moderation, not with braided hair or gold or pearls or costly clothing, but, which is proper for women professing godliness, with good works. Let a woman learn in silence with all submission. And I do not permit a woman to teach

or to have authority over a man, but to be in
silence. For Adam was formed first, then Eve.
And Adam was not deceived, but the woman being
deceived, fell into transgression. Nevertheless she
will be saved in childbearing if they continue in
faith, love, and holiness, with self-control.

1 Timothy 2:8-15 (KJV)

Have you ever read scripture, and had an "aha" moment? This happened to me while reading this text a few months ago.

Throughout the Bible, we can see that modesty is important to God. At the same time, it isn't mentioned in the same way as loving God and one another is.

Then while reading 1 Timothy 2:8-9 one day, one little phrase stuck out like it never had before...***in like manner.***

Paul is instructing us that men should pray everywhere, lifting up holy hands. He doesn't include women in this, but instead, says *in like manner* women should adorn themselves in modest apparel.

We view praying and lifting up holy hands as a form of worship, don't we? I believe that Paul is saying that the *equivalent* of men praying and lifting up holy hands is women dressing modestly, and therefore *dressing modestly is a form of worship* also. It is a form that we should uphold as very important, and that we should seek to offer to God daily.

This makes modesty so much more relevant, doesn't it?

When we consider modesty, we need to understand that we aren't given too many specifics, except for the broad terms modesty and discretion. I believe that this is to account for the many different cultures and time periods in which Christians have lived. We need to address coverage and fitment issues, but the type of clothing that fits in the modest "range" is vast. Please remember this as you read my personal testimony regarding clothing choices later. There have been times in my life (and possibly in yours) that I saw someone who is a Christian, I liked what they were doing, and so I decided to change that thing in my life because of a person. *Then* I would go to the Bible and see if it matched up. In actuality, we should seek God first, and then live our lives accordingly. .

I included 1 Timothy 2:10-15 in the text at the beginning of this short chapter since it continues to speak of a few things that are specific to women, like the instruction in modesty. This passage is controversial in our day and time. However I believe that it continues to illustrate the fact that men and women are created differently. This is not just a husband/wife issue, but is also a man/woman issue. This is not a bad thing! As I've learned more and more, I've realized just how strong and important women are in their own way.

Thoughts to Ponder

- **Have you ever related modest dress to worship before?**
- **If not, has this perspective changed how you feel about dressing modestly?**
- **Why is modesty as relevant today as it has been in the past?**
- **What is the best way to ensure we are following God's example, and not others?**

Chapter 4

Modesty Standards and the Bible

*All scripture is given by inspiration of God, and is profitable for doctrine, for reproof, for correction, **for instruction in righteousness**.*

2 Timothy 3:16 (KJV)

If you have ever read my old blog before, you probably already know that I used to wear skirts almost exclusively. Yes, even in the wintertime. (Leggings and boots made my skirts

28

so warm and comfortable). The reasons I wore either skirts or long tunics over pants were both cultural and Biblical.

While I don't wear skirts exclusively anymore since I realized how broadly Biblical interpretations can vary, I wanted to include this short chapter in this book since I know some women might find it helpful. There are many ways to look at things, and perhaps this will help you in your own study in some way.

The following verses are from Genesis 3 (ESV).

"So when the woman saw that the tree was good for food, and that it was a delight to the eyes, and that the tree was to be desired to make one wise, she took of its fruit and ate, and she also gave some to her husband who was with her, and he ate. Then the eyes of both were opened, and they knew that they were naked. **And they sewed fig leaves**

together and made themselves loincloths…And
the Lord God made for Adam and for his wife
garments of skins and clothed them."

From these verses, we can see that after the fall, Adam and Eve made clothing for themselves. This clothing was *not* sufficient in God's eyes. For women *and* men. (Men shouldn't only cover their loins, while say, swimming). From this text we can understand that what man deems as good isn't necessarily so to God in regards to dress. Also, we can see that contrary to popular opinion, God really does care about what we wear. If He didn't, the fig leaf loincloths that Adam and Eve fashioned would have been enough.

So what is God's preferred standard of dress?

Honestly, there isn't a lot to be found on this topic Biblically. But clues can be found throughout scripture regarding the type of dress that is most pleasing to God if we look carefully.

And you shall make them linen trousers to cover their nakedness; from the loins even unto the thighs they shall reach:

Exodus 28:42 (KJV)

Come down, and sit in the dust, O virgin daughter of Babylon, sit on the ground...make bare the leg, uncover the thigh, pass over the rivers. Thy nakedness shall be uncovered, yea, thy shame shall be seen. (From Isaiah 47, ESV).

From these two texts, we are encouraged to generally keep our thighs covered.

And I want women to be modest in their appearance. They should wear decent and appropriate clothing and not draw attention to themselves by the way they fix their hair or by wearing gold or pearls or expensive clothes.

1 Timothy 2:9 (NLT)

In 1 Timothy 2:9, we learn that as ladies, we should wear modest, decent, and appropriate clothing. Among other things, this means that we should be properly covered, and that it might be better for our clothing to not be form-fitting. We also should strive to not bring undue attention to ourselves by wearing over-the-top clothing or accessories...this is so our good works will shine, and not what we're wearing.

Finally, in Revelation 7, we find the clothing that God Himself chose for us to wear in Heaven.

After this I looked, and there before me was a great multitude that no one could count, from every nation, tribe, people and language, standing before the throne and before the Lamb. They were wearing white robes and were holding palm branches in their hands.

Revelation 7:9 (NIV)

In John's vision God's people are wearing long robes. Friends, to me this is the ultimate example of what perfection of dress to God might look like. Robes cover our bodies almost completely, and are not form-fitting. Throughout scripture, we find that God is our protector, and *our covering*. Covering our body with clothing mirrors what the Lord so graciously does for us.

Thoughts to Ponder

- **Do you think Biblical examples of modesty apply to our life today?**
- **What are a few Biblical clues which tell us that God really does care about what we wear?**
- **Should these examples cause us to reexamine our current clothing choices? Why or why not?**

Chapter 5

Let Your Good Works Shine

As godly women, we are called to shine.

Not to completely run this verse into to the ground, but I would really like to take a moment and concentrate on the latter part of 1 Timothy 2:8-9

I desire therefore that the men pray everywhere, lifting up holy hands, without wrath and doubting; in like manner also, that the women adorn themselves in modest apparel, with propriety and *moderation, not with braided hair or gold or pearls or costly clothing, but, which is proper for women professing godliness, **with good works**.*

1 Timothy 2:8-9 (KJV)

One of the main reasons we are instructed to dress modestly is so attention will be drawn to our good works, and not to our bodies. This instruction really flies in the face of much of what we are taught today, doesn't it?

I've been told so many times that since God looks at our heart, modesty isn't important. I've even been told that good works are not important.

But as we search God's heart, we find that good works are an important element of life. They are essential.

"If the faith that we profess is a naked faith with no evidence of works, it is not saving faith."

~R. C. Sproul

Good works are something that comes naturally if we are in complete accord with God. These good works sanctify us, and God uses them to draw others to Himself as well.

In fact, Paul says we should clothe ourselves with these good works.

If our bodies aren't properly covered, they will be competing with our good works for the attention which rightfully belongs to God.

It is so easy to be selfish, and to try to keep our clothing choices focused on our own wants and needs, instead of on the Lord's. I've been there! But over time I've found how freeing it can be to truly surrender this area of our life over to the Lord as we seek His will.

If our hearts aren't in the right place, relinquishing control of this area will be much harder to do. If we keep our desires in line with God's Word, then keeping our mind focused on our Lord and good works while making modest clothing choices will be so much easier. Matthew 6:21 states, "For where your treasure is, there your heart will be also." (NKJV) When we treasure God's instructions over everything else, clothing ourselves with proper apparel and our good works will be much simpler!

When we decide to walk with God, the old passes away and we become new. I know I touched on this earlier, but it bears repeating. Once our lives are filled with joy due to God's goodness, dressing immodestly doesn't seem as appealing anymore.

Does our beauty come from within or from our outward appearance? It comes from within, since we are daughters of the King!

"The King's daughter is all glorious within."

Psalm 45:13 (KJV)

Let's focus on this truth. It must remain in the front of our minds. When we take our eyes off of the world's standard of clothing and instead look to God, what's *within* us will shine.

Shine on!

Thoughts to Ponder

- **Besides dressing modestly, what are a few ways we can shine for God?**

- Where does our true beauty and worth come from?
- If we clothe ourselves with good works, they are evident for all to see. Can others tell that we love God simply by how we live?
- Is our immodest clothing competing with our good works?

Chapter 6

Keeping Our Eyes on God through Criticism

If you are anything like me, handling criticism can be difficult. I tend to wear not just my clothing, but also my feelings on my shoulder, which isn't exactly the best thing to do when going against the flow of our culture.

Maybe it's our friends who are critical of our modest clothing choices. Or maybe it's even our family.

I went through this when I began to dress modestly. It was tough.

In the scheme of things though, this was no big deal. But what if our husbands have a problem with our clothing choices? How should we react?

First of all, we must remember they are human too. It is so easy for them to be concerned about how others might perceive us. While the point of modesty is to blend in, sometimes modest apparel just doesn't in a sea of immodest clothing. For example, I know that I sometimes stick out while visiting a beach!

The best thing to do is sit down and talk about the concerns he may have. Sometimes the concerns are valid. And sometimes, they are not. When we talk about this issue, we need to be understanding. We also need to follow his wishes as long as they are lined up with God's ways.

Unfortunately, many husbands are intent on having "trophy wives" to show off to their friends. Let me assure you that it is never wise to flaunt our bodies in front of other men.

If our husband's wishes don't line up with the modesty standards God has impressed upon our hearts, then we should follow Him, and not our husbands.

We should have a gentle and loving spirit when we do. This can feel really hard! But we must remember that God's grace is sufficient, and we should strive to show His grace no matter what situation we are in. Usually over time, our husbands will change their minds if we handle the issue with humility and grace.

Sometimes criticism from others can seem like it's just too much to bear. When we feel this way, we must turn our eyes to God immediately and keep them there. When we are focused on

Christ, He will sustain us. This will involve us remaining focused in prayer.

Ultimately, the criticism doesn't matter so much, especially if we keep our eyes focused on God. Let's remember that dressing modestly will ultimately bless both us and those around us.

Thoughts to Ponder

- **Have you ever been criticized for wearing modest clothing?**
- **If so, how did you respond? Was your response in line with God?**
- **If our husbands don't agree with our new modest clothing choices, what should we do?**

Chapter 7

Modesty Brings Respect to Womanhood

Many years ago, modesty was commonplace. It really didn't matter if you were a believer or not, since modesty was really just a societal norm.

Over the years, this has changed.

It is so easy to flounder and feel hopeless, but we aren't to fear. We must remember that ultimately God is in control. It's all in His hands.

When we clothe ourselves in modesty, we show not only that we are willing to follow God, but also that we are His daughters who should be respected. We are more than a body to look at.

What do you believe would happen if women everywhere decided to band together and begin clothing their bodies properly? What if models began to say "no" to modeling in underwear and swimsuit ads?

I think a massive culture shift would take place.

As women, as children of God, we should be respected.

I believe with my whole heart that the Lord intends for modesty to cover us in protection. Now, we can't be in control of every thought that flies through a man's mind, especially with pornography being so rampant.

But what if we said no more to that as well?

I believe we hold the power to begin a massive culture shift if we give our lives wholeheartedly to the Lord.

I believe we hold the keys to bringing respect back to womanhood, and a large part of this respect will occur if we begin to dress modestly.

When we respect ourselves and clothe our bodies properly, others will follow.

When we start exercising discretion, others will notice.

We must be willing to make necessary changes and model modesty and discretion to the younger generation. Will you join me?

Modeling and Teaching Discretion

As I've been "recovering" modesty in my dress over the past several years, my heart has also been concerned about discretion. Discretion is also a modesty issue. You see, if we aren't discreet and bring undo attention to ourselves with our clothing, then the clothing isn't modest, no matter if it covers appropriately or not.

Let me explain.

Our clothing and accessories can definitely be pretty. Look at the world around us. It is beautiful, and is all a part of God's creation! Godliness does not equal plainness. We do not serve a boring or plain God!

That being said, I adore large earrings, and some of my tops are patterned rather wildly, or with jewels. I've felt a nudge to tone it down in these areas, and I'm slowly beginning to change my wardrobe.

While my #1 priority is to serve my God, another concern of mine is to be a good example for my daughters. Over the past few months I've had to talk "discretion" with my teenage daughter on a few occasions. Thankfully the talks have been graceful, and I haven't had any rough moments with my sixteen-year-old. We've been able to share from our hearts and appreciate what each other is saying.

A few verses that I use when discussing this topic with my daughters are:

Likewise, I want women to adorn themselves with proper clothing, modestly and discreetly, not with braided hair and gold or pearls or costly garments...1 Timothy 2:9 (NASB)

Like a gold ring in a pig's snout is a beautiful woman without discretion...Proverbs 11:22 (NIV)

While 1 Timothy 2:9 is specifically talking about discretion in dress, we should teach our daughters to be discreet in their speech and actions as well. What is the best way to do this? To model it ourselves. We cannot expect for them to be discreet if we are not first. Really, discretion is something we must focus on and learn about before we even begin to introduce the topic to our daughters.

Believe me, I am not immune to following trends without thinking about discretion first. A few years ago I was *this close* to putting a streak of pink in my hair! I thought the trend was cute, but in the end, discretion won.

Above all, we need to maintain a spirit of *grace*, since the definition of discretion will most likely vary from family to family and from culture to culture. However, it might not be the best idea to bring undue attention to ourselves. I would love it if the "rules" of discretion were more plainly spelled out for us. I believe so many women do not think of this as something applicable to today. Or they might think of discretion as an abstract quality that does not apply to appearance. But it does! Please join me in prayerfully considering this important topic. Modeling both discretion and modesty is an excellent way to bring respect back to womanhood.

Thoughts to Ponder

- **What are some ways we can bring respect back to womanhood?**
- **Do our current clothing choices indicate we respect ourselves, as well?**

- How can modest clothing offer us a form of protection?
- What are some ways we can apply discretion to our lives?

Chapter 8

A Biblical Reason to Wear Loose Clothing

For a while, my reasoning concerning wearing loose clothing was pretty much cultural, and not at all Biblically based. However, much like my sudden understanding of head covering (which I'll touch on later), I feel like God showed me a *Biblical case* for it. One reason I believe I am so intrigued by this topic is because I came from a church background in which immodest dress was considered normal and good. Those who do not share the same background as I most likely will not be as convicted about modest dress as I am.

Basically, one day I was reading some short epistles in the New Testament. I had just finished up, and then felt led to take a look at 1 Timothy. As I read verses 2:9-10 I was reminded of why modesty is so important.

In like manner also, the women adorn themselves in modest apparel, with propriety and moderation, not with braided hair or gold or pearls or costly clothing, but, which is proper for women professing godliness, with good works.

1 Timothy 2:9-10 (NKJV)

I decided to look further into the word "apparel" which is used in these verses. I've read this chapter many times before, and truly never felt any reason to look further into this before.

So, I looked into the Greek wording.

The Greek word which was translated to "apparel" or in some versions "clothing" here is **katastole.** **Katastole** is only used once in the entire Bible. There are many other Greek words that can be used for apparel, such as esthes, esthesis, himation, and himatismos. Katastole is a feminine noun. "Kata" means "a lowering, letting down." "Stole" in and of itself is not necessarily feminine, and is "a loose outer garment."

This is a more detailed description:

"According to Thayer's Lexicon, the Greek word translated "apparel" in I Timothy 2:9 (katastolē) means "a garment let down, dress, attire". The Greek word for apparel in this text is Katastole, meaning a long dress. Kata meaning down – a garment flowing down; and Stole – a long garment, covering or wrapping. It should be noted that Thayer's Lexicon describes the Greek term

stole in this way: "a loose outer garment for men which extended to the feet", and it is found in such passages as Mark 12:38 and Luke 20:46 where it is translated as "long clothing or long robes". But in I Timothy 2:9 women are commanded to adorn themselves in modest katastole, which seems to emphasize that women's legs and even feet should be covered by loose forming apparel. When women here are commanded to wear modest katastole, the term katastoleis not just a more general term for clothing, apparel, or array like the Greek term himatismos, which is translated "array" at the end of I Timothy 2:9 and apparel in Acts 20:33. The Greek word for modest is Kosmios, meaning orderly, well-arranged, decent, modest, harmonious arrangement, or adornment. Modesty is also Biblically applied to one's demeanor or behavior. This same Greek word is translated good behavior in 1 Timothy 3:2 in the qualifications of bishops. Therefore, women are instructed to wear modest long dresses (Kosmios Katastole). Thus this Kosmios Katastole not only *specifies that the article of clothing should be a dress, but also specifies that the dress should be of a suitably long length. And I Timothy 2:9 teaches that this dress is to be characterized by "shamefacedness" and "sobriety".* (from http://www.puritans.net)

Sometimes, it is easy to dismiss Biblical teachings as strictly cultural. For example, we can look at many of the times that the word "apparel" is used in the Bible and say, that's what people used to wear, and it no longer applies to us. When we read about what Bible characters were wearing, this can be true. But the verses in 1 Timothy are written in more of an instructional form.

Thoughts to Ponder

- **Do you believe God would like for us to cover our bodies in flowing** garments today? Why or why not?

- Do you believe the Greek word "katastole" applies to us today when we make clothing choices?

Chapter 9

A Conversation About Headcovering

Headcovering. While Paul spends a good bit of time discussing them, whenever I read the 11th chapter of 1 Corinthians, I usually walk away terribly confused. However, I believe my eyes have been opened to something in this passage that I have never seen before, and I am just bursting to share it with you in this chapter. (*Hint*: It doesn't have much to do with headship, and everything to do with God's glory).

My "view" of headcoverings has changed over my life. When I was a teenager, I was taught that the entire passage was cultural, and had absolutely no place in our life today. I was told that in Corinth, only harlots wore their hair uncovered, so it was unbecoming for Christian women to do so during that time. At the same time, men in *our* culture regularly remove hats during worship and prayer. I was confused by the double standard. As a young adult, I believed a covering *was* called for, but that this covering was long hair in women.

Let me step back for a moment, and share the passage in question with you.

Imitate me, just as I also imitate Christ. Now I praise you, brethren, that you remember me in all things and keep the traditions just as I delivered them to you. But I want you to know that the head of every man is Christ, the head of woman is man, and the head of Christ is God.

Every man praying or prophesying, having his head covered, dishonors his head. But every woman who prays or prophesies with her head uncovered dishonors her head, for that is one and the same as if her head were shaved. For if a woman is not covered, let her also be shorn. But if it is shameful for a woman to be shorn or shaved, let her be covered. For a man indeed ought not to cover his head, since he is the image and glory of God; but woman is the glory of man. For man is not from woman, but woman from man. Nor was man created for the woman, but woman for the man. For this reason the woman ought to have a symbol of authority on her head, because of the angels. Nevertheless, neither is man independent of woman, nor woman independent of man, in the Lord. For as woman came from man, even so man also comes through woman; but all things are from God. Judge among yourselves. Is it proper for a woman to pray to God with her head uncovered? Does not even nature itself teach you that if a man has long hair, it is a dishonor to him?

But if a woman has long hair, it is a glory to her; for her hair is given to her for a covering. But if anyone seems to be contentious, we have no such custom, nor do the churches of God. ~1 Corinthians 11:1-16 (NKJV)

You see, I took the words, *"But if a woman has long hair, it is a glory to her; for her hair is given to her for a covering,"* as meaning "long hair fulfills all of the confusing requirements above." Also, verse 16 wiped away the requirement in its entirety if there was "contention" (or so I thought).

Although this passage of scripture was still a puzzle to me, through study I figured out a few of the pieces.

1. Paul did not say the reason to cover is to distinguish the ladies of the Corinthian church from the harlots in town. I

believe if that was the reason, he would have said it. Instead, he appeals to the *creation order and angels* as the reasoning behind head coverings. I would say these are reasons that are still in place today.

2. While studying, verse 6 really sounded like hair was not the intended head covering. *"For if a woman is not covered, let her also be shorn. But if it is shameful for a woman to be shorn or shaved, let her be covered."* It wouldn't make sense if the "covered" in this verse meant "hair". For example, *"For if a woman does not have long hair, let her also be shorn"*. If she didn't have long hair, she

would already be shorn. This just didn't make sense to me.

3. While the KJV and NKJV, says that "*if anyone is contentious, we have no such custom*," a few other versions such as the NASB say, "*if anyone is contentious, we have no other custom*". The use of "other" made so much more sense to me. Before I would wonder, "Why would Paul spend so much time on the topic, just to say, "never mind if you don't want to."

Given these discoveries, several months ago I decided to make a couple of wide headbands and purchase a few hats to begin wearing to worship. (These verses are in a section where Paul is discussing public worship). I was still puzzled, still confused, but I thought if this was something the Lord *might possibly* want me to do, then I should do it. It is a little thing, but I want to be obedient in the little *and* big things!

Up until this point, the only arguments I had heard concerning covering was about it being a sign of headship. While it is true that covering is a sign of headship, it is also so much more.

Are you still with me? I hope that I haven't lost you, I am getting to what in my opinion is the really important part.

Months ago I began subscribing to a site called The Head Covering Movement. (Yes, my husband has teased me for this, ha!) Anyhow, while reading their articles and blog posts I began to piece a few clues together that made this passage become clear to me.

- *Clue #1 Paul used two completely separate Greek*

words for "covering" in the
passage.

The 'covering' mentioned in verses 4 and 5 is katakalupto which means to veil, cover up one's self. The 'covering' in verse 15 is peribolaion which means to wrap around (as in peri-meter).

Why would Paul have used two different words if he meant the same covering?

Now the verses began to become clearer to me. Sometimes the English language doesn't translate exactly right, and we must go back to the Greek. Paul wasn't talking about hair in the beginning of the passage. He was specifically instructing women to cover their hair with a veil. But why?

- ***Clue #2 It is all about God's glory.***

Okay y'all, this is the most important part. I do not know how I have missed this as many times as I have read this passage.

When we are praying and prophesying in public worship, who should get the glory? Where should *all* of the glory fall? To God.

If we look back to 1 Corinthians, we see that in verse 7 "*women are the glory of man.*" Not God. Now let's look at verse 15 again, which is the verse where many of us become confused and declare that our hair is enough.

But if a woman has long hair, it is a glory to her;
for her hair is given to her for a covering.

1 Corinthians 11:15 (NASB)

So…while long hair is a "covering" given by nature, it is a glory to…us. I believe Paul is instructing us to cover our *peribolaion* (hair covering) with a *katakalupto* (physical covering, like a veil or hat) so that all glory will flow to God during worship. I also better understand why some women choose to cover full-time, and I totally respect that.

As you know, I'm a big advocate for modest dress. I've been known to say that men cannot pay full attention to the worship service if the women around them are wearing short skirts and low-cut tops. Why is this? *Because women are the glory of man.* In the same way, I believe Paul is telling us that *our hair is our very own glory, and that this should be covered during worship as well.* Because when it comes to glory, God deserves it all!

Earlier in 1 Corinthians, Paul instructed us that *no flesh should glory in His presence.* (1 Corinthians 1:27) Our physical bodies and hair are parts of our flesh.

From http://www.bcchapel.org/questions/HeadCovering s1Cor11.html:

"Notice the references in verses 7 & 15 to glory. When the church comes together as a congregation to worship God, whose glory do we want to see? Man's glory? Or God's glory? The Apostle Paul tells us in 1st Corinthians 1:27 "But God has chosen the foolish things of the world to put to shame the wise, and God has chosen the weak things of the world to put to shame the things which are mighty; and the base things of the world and the things which are despised God has chosen, and the things which are not, to bring to nothing the things that are, that no flesh should glory in His presence." *Think about the implications of this.*

When we gather as a congregation to worship God, His glory is paramount, and our glory needs to disappear, get hidden, and be out of sight. We

70

don't need to see any sort of human glory in God's presence, the only glory seen in the church meeting ought to be the glory of Christ. Whether a person covers or uncovers their head depends on whose glory they want to be displayed."

Since a woman's hair *is* her glory, it cannot be the covering *of* her glory.

Also, I have always wondered why a covering *would not* be necessary if a woman's hair was cut short. If it was a simple symbol of headship, why should it matter if a woman had hair or not? A woman is still a woman regardless of her hair length... *For if a woman is not covered, let her also be shorn. But if it is shameful for a woman to be shorn or shaved, let her be covered (1 Corinthians 11:6).* I believe that Paul wrote this since if a woman's hair (glory) is cut short or shaved, there is no longer any need to cover it in the presence of God, since it has lost its glory.

I think that I better understand verse 10 as well now, which has always been a *complete* mystery to me!

For this reason the woman ought to have a symbol of authority on her head, because of the angels.

1 Corinthians 11:10 (NKJV)

Why should women wear a headcovering because of the angels? *Because angels are in the business of glorifying God!* Angels are present during our worship, and wouldn't they want to see *all* glory going to God, and not the least bit going to ourselves?

I am beyond thrilled that a "mystery passage" of scripture has been made plain to me. If you have ever been confused about this passage, or have contemplated head coverings, I hope this information has helped.

Thoughts to Ponder

- Have your thoughts about head covering changed after reading this chapter? Why or why not?
- What are a few ways we can keep our flesh from displaying glory in God's presence?
- While in public worship, where should all the glory fall?

Chapter 10

Are You Ready to Suit Up?

In summer, swimming pools and beach getaways are par for the course. Which means we need to begin purchasing swimwear. Is this something ladies and girls need to even really consider? Should we just run to the store and purchase the cutest suit regardless of its fabric coverage?

My goal isn't to tell you what is "right and wrong," because honestly, when it comes to modesty sometimes the area is very grey. But some questions and topics that I hope to cover quickly include:

- The History of Swimwear. Where were we then, and where are we now?
- Are We Letting Our Culture or God Dictate Our Convictions?
- Practical Ways to Remain Modest While Swimming and Links to Resources to Buying Modest Suits.

In the early 1920s, swimsuits would be measured on the beach. If the suits were too short, the women would be fined.

We've come a long way, haven't we?

So, are you ready to take a quick look at the history of swimwear? Swimming has been a popular pastime for centuries. Who wouldn't want a refreshing dip on a hot day? Hopefully during this study we will discover how throughout history swim wear has evolved from modesty-focused suits to suits that are made for the express purpose of exposing the body. As women, this topic is important.

Let's start hundreds of years ago. In the 1700s, "bathing gowns" were what ladies wore to swim in. They were made of weighted fabric that did not rise in the water. Modesty was very important, and ladies and men did not swim together. Women rarely swam at all actually, for modesty's sake.

In the early 1800s, swimming became an important form of recreation in the United States. The "Princess cut" suit was introduced, which included a long blouse and pants in one piece. Women still refrained from swimming too much, for fear of being immodest.

In 1909, Australian Annette Kellerman was arrested in the United States for wearing a one piece suit which included shorts. By 1910, the general public accepted this style of swimsuit. By 1918, the apron that was worn with swimsuits disappeared.

This is when swimwear styles really began to move from being modesty-focused to being focused on body shape.

In the 1940s, Hollywood actresses began wearing swimsuits in motion pictures. They became tighter fitting and higher cut.

In 1946, French engineer Louis Reard created the bikini. He named it after the nuclear tests at Bikini Atoll, because it arrived with a "bang." When he created the bikini none of the "regular" models would wear it. He finally hired 19-year-old nude dancer Micheline Bernardini to model the suit.

From this point forward, swimsuits continued to become smaller and smaller. They became less about modesty and function, and more about showing off the body.

In our current day and age, we rarely consider why we wear certain things. Our clothing and swimsuit styles are fueled by current trends without giving much thought as to if these "trends" are glorifying God or not.

So, where do we go from here? This topic can be so very confusing in regards to modesty. On one hand, it's so easy to go with the flow of cultural influences and wear what everyone else is wearing without really giving it much thought. On the other hand, some Christians do not swim with mixed-gender groupings, or wear a suit that basically covers them from head to toe. What is a woman to do?

First of all, I would like to say that we all will look at this subject differently. This is totally okay! If our modesty choices are made beside a flourishing walk with God, then we will have made the right choice for ourselves. So secondly, it is important to pray about this. It might seem like a silly topic to pray about, but modesty is important, and can affect our walk with God and others.

After spending time with God in prayer, let's answer the following questions:

What does fabric coverage have to do with it?

This is when most people begin talking about bikinis. They say, *"If you would not wear your bra and underwear in public, why would you wear a bikini?"* This is a valid point! But I'd like to take it one step further.

But what if in "normal" life you truly feel like your shirt must have sleeves? Or that your legs should be covered to your knees? If this is so, please do not compromise your modesty standards just to go swimming. There are swimwear alternatives that will work for you.

What does age have to do with it?

If we have a close walk with God, it is good to model appropriate dress for other women who are younger than us and for our daughters. They are learning from us *now*, and what we allow them to wear at a young age will affect their perception of modesty throughout their entire lives.

Why all the rules?

Honestly, there aren't many cut and dry rules here. My hope is that we will all look to God instead of our culture when we choose our swimwear. If you would normally not wear certain things in public, then swimming is not an excuse to do so. Yes, our culture does influence our choice of colors, fabrics, and styles, but let's not let it influence our choice of coverage.

If you've decided to purchase a modest swimsuit, where do you turn next? Being modest while swimming is something that *can* be done, but sometimes it comes with a higher price tag. For me and my family, it is worth it! We usually shop in the active wear section, and purchase shorts and rash guards for the girls. I also wear leggings underneath my swim skirt.

What is the simplest way to get more coverage out of a bathing suit?

Probably the easiest and cheapest way would be to add swim shorts or a swim skirt to a one-piece with a high cut neckline. Some ladies desire even more coverage however.

Where can I purchase swimwear with more coverage?

The following are some online resources that might be helpful in your search:

http://www.undercoverwaterwear.com/

http://hydrochic.com/

http://www.wholesomewear.com/

http://modestsea.com/

http://www.meanttobemodest.com/

http://www.sunwayuvclothing.com/

http://aquamodesta.com/

I hope these resources have been helpful. Best wishes if you decide to look for a modest swimsuit.

Thoughts to Ponder

- **Do our current swimsuit choices match our "everyday" modesty standards?**
- **If not, do you think it would be pleasing to God if they did?**
- **Do you think the history of swimsuits should affect our swimsuit choices now? Why or why not?**
- **Do you think it would be worth our while to spend the time and resources needed to make our swimsuits more modest?**

Chapter 11

My Modesty Journey

Everyone's story is different, and this is mine. I hope it is encouraging to you.

I was my parents' first child in 1980. At that time we lived in northwest Indiana. I do not remember much about my family's modesty standards during this time, but what I *do* remember is that we were not active in church. My family was Catholic, but we did not attend mass.

Fast forward a few years...my family of four (I now had a little brother) decided to spend a month vacationing in Atlanta. My dad's sister lived there, and they were going out of town during this time. Their family always intrigued me. My aunt had converted to the Baha'i faith when she married my uncle, and they appeared very devout. We had a great month in the South, and spent a good deal of time at their pool. My cousin's clothing and bathing suit choices were mainstream, so it never really occurred to me that clothing choices might vary depending on one's faith.

Our family loved this vacation so much that my parents decided to make a *permanent* move to the Atlanta area. I was six years old, and was excited beyond belief at the prospect of no more long winters! Since we were moving to a warmer climate, that meant we would be wearing less clothing as well. I remember going through my mother's closet in elementary school, and finding this shirt that I just *had* to wear. It was a tank top, but the front was gathered from top to bottom and cinched together at the chest so her midriff would show. Of course she wouldn't let me wear it, but I remember the shirt to this day. It had such a "cool" factor. My mother did not dress modestly, and I wanted to be just like her.

I attended elementary school in the 80's, and fashion was definitely interesting, while modesty was not a priority. My clothes were definitely tight and bright! While going skating or to Six Flags, I wanted to wear more provocative clothing than what was allowed in school. My favorite outfit included spandex covered in extremely short ripped denim shorts. I shake my head now just thinking about it. But honestly, I wasn't taught otherwise.

By this time it was the early 90's, and my family was looking for a church home. We landed at an Evangelical Methodist church, and I loved it so much. I had attended church with my friends and gone to Vacation Bible School in the past, but this was the first time I had attended an actual service that was more than fun and games with a Bible lesson wrapped inside. At that time, God spoke to my heart concerning being more discreet. I was twelve years old. I told my mom that all I wanted to wear were Christian t-shirts and jeans. She was happy about my new relationship with Jesus, but didn't really know how to lead me differently concerning modesty. I was still wearing skin tight jeans, and attended public school. I begged, and begged, and begged some more to either be homeschooled, or enrolled in a Christian school. The way other children acted, dressed and talked just hurt my spirit immensely. After a year of pleading, I grew tired of not having many friends (since my conversion I had lost a ton), and decided that if I was going to survive the next five years I would need to somewhat fit in. I tried out for cheerleading in the 8th grade and made the squad.

The year was 1994 when I made the 8th grade cheerleading squad. I was *very* excited, but looking back now, this was one of the worst decisions I ever made. To me, it marks the beginning of a falling away from God, and a struggle with sin that would last almost a decade. Our skirts were short, and we rolled them up to make them even shorter. In the 9th grade our competitive cheerleading squad purchased skirts without pleats for the first time ever. I still remember the controversy today. Our coach fought tooth and nail for those skirts, and they finally were approved. We were only allowed to wear them on campus *if* we wore our warm up pants underneath.

In the 10th grade I was named Homecoming Princess for my grade level, and by the 11th grade, I was tired of it all. I stopped caring so much about being "popular," but did still dress immodestly. This included midriff baring tops, very short skirts, etc. It was the norm; everyone dressed this way. I attended church, but modesty was not taught in the least. My parents had decided to move from the church of my conversion to a charismatic church when I was in the 8th grade as well, and my relationship with God suffered during the change.

It wasn't until my first daughter was born when I was nearly 20 that I really decided to take a look at my clothing choices. I wanted to look like a mother, not a *teenager.* Everyone said that I looked young for my age to begin with, so I wanted to dress a bit more conservatively. At this point I made sure that my midriff was covered, and my skirts were at least mid-thigh in length. My swimsuit choices were still very poor, however. I did it for me so *I* would feel better about how *others* saw me. I still did none of this for my God.

I met my amazing husband when I was 23. My first husband had passed away, and I was living by myself with three young children. Around that time, I really wanted to restore my relationship with God. I really *yearned* to seek the Lord, but still was holding onto the world.

After my husband and I were married, our girls began dancing competitively. I really had no clue what we were getting into at that point, since I had danced competitively as a child and really enjoyed it. The costumes were *so* immodest, and while they somewhat bothered me, they *really* bothered my husband. Over time, we both became convicted about allowing our daughters to dress in such a way, even if it was just on stage. Soon after, we switched the dance school our daughters attended.

We *still* dressed immodestly for the most part unfortunately. God was slowly working on my heart though. It is truly amazing how the Lord works. My conscience began working in overdrive while shopping for clothing, and I didn't even really understand why! I began to purchase one piece or tankini bathing suits for my daughters and myself instead of bikinis. I bought long shorts instead of short shorts. I made sure that our necklines were not low cut for the first time ever. This wasn't something the church taught us, but I just knew in my heart that dressing modestly was pleasing to my God.

I desperately wanted to walk in God's truth, and I began to read books that taught about modesty.

Through one of these books, I learned about a few shops that sold modest clothing and I visited it with much excitement on my next trip to town. Since then, I've not looked back!

Thoughts to Ponder

- **Okay, enough about me. Now, I would love for you to think about your own clothing choices...your own modesty**

transformation if you will. If you believe God would like for you to make some changes in your clothing, I would love to encourage you to be obedient. There is such joy to be found in obedience!

In Conclusion

I hope these short chapters have given you some food for thought. Modesty can let our light shine for God. When we look to Him, we won't be left wanting. God will lead the way, and we will experience the true joy which follows having a close walk with Him.

Above all, yearn for God. Seek Him. Everything else will fall into place.

About the Author

NICOLE CRONE enjoys writing both fiction and nonfiction books. Her book for moms, 31 Days of Rest: Daily Thoughts for Tired Moms, is a guide for moms who are looking for rest in their daily lives. Nicole has been a contributing writer at Year Round Homeschooling, and her articles have been featured at For Every Mom. When Nicole isn't homeschooling her children, you can find her writing, reading, sewing, or gardening.

Made in the USA
Columbia, SC
02 June 2025

58786560R00052